The Priory of St Pancras Lewes

By Arthur Franklin

Edited by Kate Hickmott and Anthony Freeman

G000123966

The Priory of St Pancras, Lewes, was once a holy site. For nearly 500 years men lived here to pray, in obedience to rules laid down by St Benedict in the 6th century. All Christians believed that their life on earth was a preparation for life after death whether in hell or heaven. The monks were convinced that their austere way of life guaranteed them eternal salvation. The monks lived within a walled enclosure away from the people of Lewes, though some of the monks did have to have contact with the outside world.

Every Day the Work of God

St Benedict based this "horarium" on the Old Testament - Psalm 119: "at midnight I will rise to give thanks unto thee" and "seven times a day do I praise thee". As a year passed the times changed with the hours of daylight but the sequence remained the same.

"Idleness is the enemy of the soul" *St Benedict*

IN THE DORMITORY SLEEPING FULLY DRESSED

"After Compline no one is allowed to say anything" *St Benedict*

Midnight · 1am · 2am · 3am · 4am · 5am · 6am · 7am · 8am · 9am · 10am · 11am · Noon · 1pm · 2pm · 3pm · 4pm · 5pm · 6pm · 7pm · 8pm · 9pm · 10pm · 11pm

Out of bed and process to church
Psalms, readings and prayers
CHURCH - *Nocturns*

Toilet break REREDORTER

Psalms and hymns
CHURCH - *Matins*

Psalms and readings
CHURCH - *Prime*

Reading CLOISTER

Putting on day shoes DORMITORY
Washing LAVATORIUM
Psalms and readings
CHURCH - *Terce*

Mass for the dead CHURCH

Meeting of all monks
CHAPTER HOUSE

Intellectual, artistic or some manual work
CLOISTER (or elsewhere)

Psalms and readings
CHURCH - *Sext*

High Mass CHURCH

Psalms and prayers
CHURCH - *None*

Eating REFECTORY

Reading or other tasks
CLOISTER (or elsewhere)

Psalms and hymns
CHURCH - *Vespers*

Light refreshment
REFECTORY

Psalms and readings
CHURCH - *Compline*

In bed sleeping fully clothed
DORMITORY

"Two dishes will suffice for the daily meal. Nothing is more contrary than over-indulgence." *St Benedict*

"Any brother who does not apply himself to his reading is useless to himself and a distraction to others" *St Benedict*

© Andy Gammon / Anthony Freeman

The life of a monastery

A monk's life

The monks and their prior followed the Rule of St Benedict with its rigorous daily ritual of devotions. A book now in the Fitzwilliam Museum in Cambridge (the late 13th century Lewes Breviary) sets out the daily celebrations and masses for saints, martyrs and benefactors performed in the church and its many chapels. The monks regularly processed through the cloister and into the Great Church where they attended eight services each day and night with additional services on important festivals such as Easter and major saints' days. Services were often sung without any musical accompaniment. This is known as plainsong. Services to remember the dead, particularly of the Priory and its benefactors, were important.

The number of monks varied from the four monks who came from France to establish the Priory to the hundred who were claimed to be present in 1240, falling to the 24 who were in residence at the time of the dissolution. Young men joined the community as novices. They were taught to read and write Latin - the language in which most religious texts were written. On joining the Priory they took vows of poverty, chastity and obedience. They followed the very strict rule of silence enforced in the monastery, speaking only during short designated periods in the day and communicating at other times by a form of sign language, though by the 13th century there were complaints that the monks were using sign language to chatter too much! On weekdays speaking was only allowed for half an hour in the morning and half an hour in the evening and silence was kept all day on Sunday and on special religious days. The Rule prescribed what the monks could eat and initially did not allow them meat, except when they were ill. However, over the centuries the rules were relaxed and meat was more regularly consumed and an extra glass of wine allowed on special occasions. Cluniac monks wore black wool robes covered by a black floor-length cloak with a hood. They had two pairs of day shoes and one pair of night boots lined with fur. They were not

13th century Lewes Breviary, probably produced at the Priory. It included a mass for the patron saint, St Pancras.
© Fitzwilliam Museum

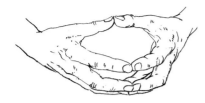

Bread

Cheese

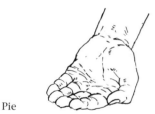

Pie

Examples of signs used to indicate food. Sometimes the signs could be combined to say, for example, "cheese pie".

allowed any other possessions except for a wooden comb, a writing tablet and a knife to cut food. Monks were clean shaven with a tonsure (the crown of the head was shaved). Every monastery needed books and monks spent much time making new copies by hand. A small writing tool was among finds made by archaeologists at the Priory. It is known that in the 13th century the Priory had its own school where John Peckham, Archbishop of Canterbury from 1279 to 1292, was educated.

Life at the Priory was tightly organised and monks were allocated responsibilities to ensure the smooth running of the community. The most important position was that of prior. He had overall control. He was the spiritual head of the community and needed to be an astute business manager as benefactors gave the Priory vast estates in Sussex, Yorkshire and Norfolk and rights over numerous churches. In the early 14th century priors of Lewes often attended parliament. They were also regularly occupied in the supervision of the six English Cluniac priories that were under the control of Lewes Priory. Both the abbot of Cluny and the Warennes were involved in appointing priors at Lewes and until the end of the fourteenth century most of the priors were of French origin. In 1377 the French-born prior of Lewes was captured resisting a French raiding force at Rottingdean. His ransom cost the Priory more than a year's income.

Other positions of responsibility were allocated to monks at the Priory. The sub-prior ran the Priory during the prior's frequent absences. The chamberlain acted as the accountant and supervised all financial transactions. The provost was in charge of punishment, ensuring that the monks followed the many rules. The cellarer was responsible for keeping all the food needed for the monks and the sacristan looked after the church and the candles. Many other roles were assigned to the monks ranging from connestabulus (responsible for looking after the horses) to almoner (in charge of giving food to the poor).

The history of the site

The first Cluniac Priory in Britain

This priory was founded between 1078 and 1082 by William de Warenne and his wife Gundrada. William was a baron who had fought alongside William the Conqueror at the battle of Hastings. Vast estates in Sussex, Surrey, Norfolk and Yorkshire were his reward and the castle which he built in Lewes, though now much changed, still dominates the skyline.

In 1076, so it is believed, William and Gundrada visited the abbey of Cluny, in France. The monks at Cluny gave great emphasis to prayer and devotion especially for the souls of the dead. They had little time for manual labour. William and Gundrada were so impressed that they eventually persuaded abbot Hugh, and William the Conqueror, to send four monks to Lewes. Hugh appointed Lanzo, noted for his holiness, to be the first prior, and Warenne gave the monks a small Saxon church in Southover which he had "recently converted from wood to stone". This little church was already dedicated to St Pancras and Warenne now gave it enough land and income to support twelve monks.

From this humble beginning the Priory of St Pancras - just one among hundreds of Cluniac monasteries in western Europe - became the most important Cluniac foundation in England. It went on to create its own 'family' by founding daughter monasteries such as Castle Acre in Norfolk and Monks Horton in Kent. Other Cluniac priories, among them Wenlock, in Shropshire, Pontefract in Yorkshire, and Paisley and Crossraguel in Scotland, were also established in Britain, though they were not directly linked to Lewes. For hundreds of years the priors at Lewes answered to the abbot of Cluny and all Cluniac monks made their vows to him either in France or on one of his rare visits abroad. However, Cluny's control gradually weakened and in 1480 the pope made Lewes Priory fully independent.

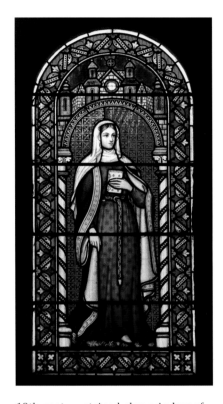

19th century stained glass window of Gundrada, from the Gundrada Chapel, St John the Baptist Church, Lewes. She is pictured with a view of the Priory above her.   Lewes Priory Trust

The Lewes link with Cluny

The Abbey of Cluny, in France, was founded in 910. By the 12th century Cluny controlled a network of over a thousand priories throughout western Europe. The co-founders of the Priory of St Pancras, Lewes, were William and Gundrada de Warenne. They visited Cluny in 1076 and persuaded the Abbot to send them a Prior and 3 monks to establish the Priory in Lewes. It became the first Cluniac House in Britain.

The Priory of St Pancras came to own extensive estates throughout England, and founded several daughter houses. The Cluniac Order was known for the splendour and length of its church services as well as the artistic quality and decoration of its religious buildings.

Key
- Lewes daughter houses in England
- Other Cluniac houses

SCOTLAND
Paisley
Crossraguel

Arthington
Pontefract
Kersall
Monk Bretton
Lenton
Norman's Burrow
Derby
Broomholm
Wenlock
Castle Acre
Witchingham
Dudley
Alderman's Haw
Mendham
WALES
Thetford
Wangford
Clifford
Northampton
Horkesley
St. Clears
Daventry
Newton Longville
Malpas
Stanesgate
ENGLAND
Prittlewell
Monkton Farleigh
Bermondsey
Barnstaple
Montacute
Monks Horton
Exeter
Kerswell
LEWES
FLANDERS
St. Cyriacus
St. Helen

THE CHANNEL

GERMANY

NORMANDY
PARIS (St.Martin)

BRITTANY

FRANCE
La Charité
BURGUNDY
Souvigny
CLUNY

BAY OF BISCAY

GUYENNE

Major extensions were underway from the 1170s and well into the next century, work which proved costly. Over the centuries the financial fortunes of the Priory fluctuated. Throughout the 13th and 14th centuries successive priors struggled to reduce the Priory's considerable debts, but with only limited and occasional success. However the situation had improved by the early 16th century when, according to the national survey of church property (the *Valor Ecclesiasticus* of 1535, compiled on the orders of Henry VIII's chief minister Thomas Cromwell), Lewes Priory had a gross annual income of £1,091 9s 6d (which could be well in excess of £5 million today). This made it the richest of the seventeen religious houses in Sussex. Like all other monasteries in England and Wales its life was brought to an end by Henry VIII.

Examples of decorated and glazed floor tiles found at the Priory site, now housed at the British Museum, London, Anne of Cleves House and Barbican House Museum, Lewes.

The first church

St Pancras, the patron Saint of the Priory, detail from the brass of Prior Thomas Nelond now in St Peter's Church, Cowfold.
Lewes Priory Trust

The Priory and the Battle of Lewes

On at least two occasions the Priory received royal visitors. In the 12th century King Stephen attended the consecration of the Priory. Over a hundred years later King Henry III arrived unexpectedly on May 12th 1264 with his army to prepare for a battle against his barons. May 12th was the feast day of St Pancras and so a special occasion for the monks of the Priory. The arrival of the king and his army caused a great deal of inconvenience and cost to the monks, who had to house and feed them all at a time when the Priory was already full of important guests who had come to celebrate the feast. Two days later Henry's army was defeated by Simon de Montfort at the Battle of Lewes. Henry was forced to retreat to the Priory where he surrendered and signed a document, the Mise of Lewes. No copies of the document survive and there has been debate over what it contained.

However Simon de Montfort's victory at Lewes in 1264 led to the summoning of a Parliament which included, for the first time, elected representatives from the shires and towns. Thus Lewes can rightly be associated with the creation of Parliament as an institution where the views of the elected representatives of the people where heard for the first time.

The fabric of the Priory church suffered damage when de Montfort's troops fired flaming arrows at the retreating King's soldiers. Many were killed in the battle. During excavations to lay the railway in the mid-nineteenth century, a burial pit to the east of the Great Church was discovered which contained hundreds of bodies. According to the geologist Gideon Mantell, it took 13 railway wagons to remove them.

Right: Lewes town, the castle and the Priory circa 1500

Left: the Battle of Lewes is commemorated by Enzo Plazzotta's Helmet, erected in 1964 to mark the 700 year anniversary of the Battle of Lewes. The frieze depicts stories about the battle from The Song of Lewes, a long Latin poem by an unknown churchman. This section shows the monks looking on in disapproval as the king's soldiers abuse their hospitality before the battle. If you look through the slits in the Helmet you can see Lewes Castle.

The buildings

The Church 21, 1

The monks used the church Warenne had given them and enlarged it. It was decorated with frescoes of high quality and was completed in the 1090s. Warenne wanted to be buried here, beside his wife (who had died in childbirth at Castle Acre). Later their remains were reburied in the Priory's Chapter House. 5 By the time Warenne died in 1088 the original community had grown to 12 monks and was still expanding. Work had begun on the planned Great Church 1. This work was still in progress when the church was consecrated on St Pancras' Day (May 12th) 1146 in a spectacular ceremony conducted by Theobold, Archbishop of Canterbury, in the presence of King Stephen and his brother Henry of Blois the Bishop of Winchester. Column bases from the south-west tower of the Great Church suggest that at least the foundations and part of the nave had been laid, but the towers were still under construction in 1268. The layout and style of decoration of the Great Church closely followed that of the Abbey of Cluny, with double transepts and five chapels surrounding the eastern apse. One of these chapels, dedicated to the Virgin, is known to have been completed by 1229. Exquisite wall paintings and ornately carved stone capitals adorned the church to the glory of God. Warenne's church may have then become the chapel for the nearby infirmary 22.

Carved stone capital (top part of a pillar). Each of the four faces of the capital are carved with a different scene from the life of St Peter. Two faces are shown below
© Trustees of the British Museum

Carved stone capital showing a griffin and a lion
© Trustees of the British Museum

The development of the site

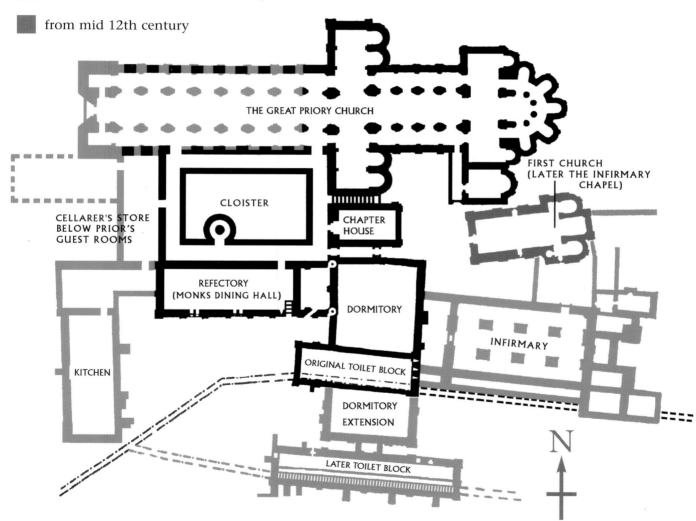

from c.1080

from late 11th to mid 12th century

from mid 12th century

THE GREAT PRIORY CHURCH

FIRST CHURCH
(LATER THE INFIRMARY
CHAPEL)

CLOISTER

CELLARER'S STORE
BELOW PRIOR'S
GUEST ROOMS

CHAPTER
HOUSE

REFECTORY
(MONKS DINING HALL)

DORMITORY

INFIRMARY

KITCHEN

ORIGINAL TOILET BLOCK

DORMITORY
EXTENSION

LATER TOILET BLOCK

N

11

This is a reconstruction of the Great Church as it might have looked just before demolition in 1538. It is based on the description by Giovanni Portinari in 1538 and on the results of excavations. The view is looking east along the nave of the Great Church, with Christ in Majesty painted above the high altar.

Portinari's measurements

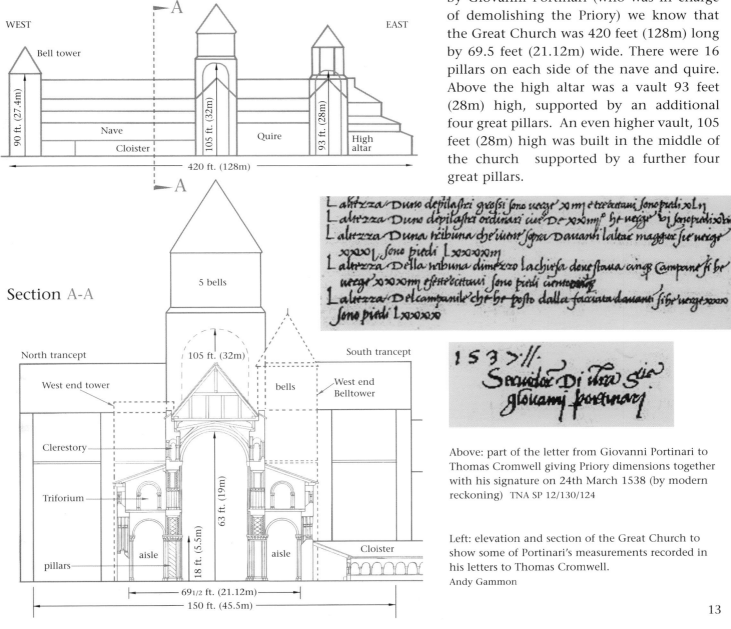

WEST

Bell tower

90 ft. (27.4m)

Nave

Cloister

105 ft. (32m)

Quire

93 ft. (28m)

High altar

EAST

420 ft. (128m)

Section A-A

5 bells

North trancept

105 ft. (32m)

South trancept

West end tower

bells

West end Belltower

Clerestory

Triforium

pillars

63 ft. (19m)

18 ft. (5.5m)

aisle

aisle

Cloister

69½ ft. (21.12m)

150 ft. (45.5m)

From exact measurements recorded in 1538 by Giovanni Portinari (who was in charge of demolishing the Priory) we know that the Great Church was 420 feet (128m) long by 69.5 feet (21.12m) wide. There were 16 pillars on each side of the nave and quire. Above the high altar was a vault 93 feet (28m) high, supported by an additional four great pillars. An even higher vault, 105 feet (28m) high was built in the middle of the church supported by a further four great pillars.

Above: part of the letter from Giovanni Portinari to Thomas Cromwell giving Priory dimensions together with his signature on 24th March 1538 (by modern reckoning) TNA SP 12/130/124

Left: elevation and section of the Great Church to show some of Portinari's measurements recorded in his letters to Thomas Cromwell.

Andy Gammon

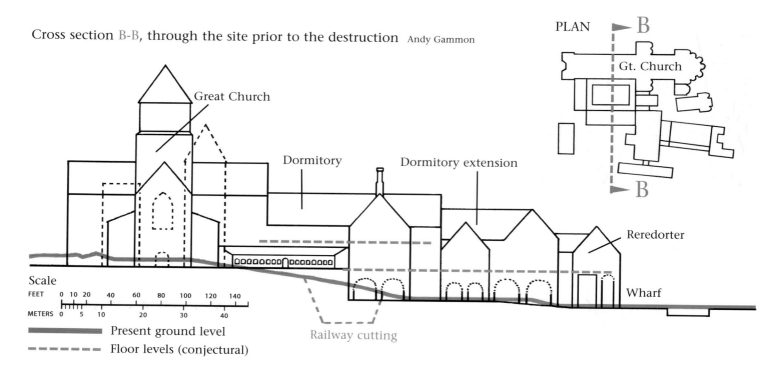

Cross section B-B, through the site prior to the destruction Andy Gammon

PLAN ▶ B

Gt. Church

▶ B

Great Church

Dormitory

Dormitory extension

Reredorter

Wharf

Railway cutting

Scale

FEET   0 10 20   40   60   80   100   120   140

METERS 0   5   10   20   30   40

━━━━━ Present ground level

- - - - - - Floor levels (conjectural)

Dorter 4 (Monks' dormitory)

As you walk around the site you will notice that the Priory's builders had to cope with different ground levels. The slope of the site meant that the original dorter (dormitory) 4 was built at a higher level than the adjoining reredorter (toilet block) 9. On the upper floor of the original dormitory there were sleeping quarters for at least twelve monks and initially the prior in an unheated open-plan room. Monks slept on simple straw mattresses but individual cubicles might have been put in later and the prior moved to his own lodgings. A warming room, 6 probably below the dormitory, provided one of the few heated rooms in the Priory (apart from the kitchen and the infirmary). At night the monks used stairs to the cloister 2 to reach the church for their devotions.

The dormitory on the first floor with an undercroft beneath.

Original reredorter 9 (Original toilet block)

Attached to this dormitory (at right angles) was a toilet block, which possibly included a small bath house. There were ten toilets in arched cubicles, set into the walls. Chutes underneath channelled the waste into a vaulted sewer below. The sewer can still be seen at the western end. Ventilation was provided by small openings at floor level.

The increasing number of monks meant that a bigger dormitory and toilet block became necessary and so in the late 12th century the dormitory was extended through the existing toilet block and a new larger toilet block constructed further south.

Below left: the 11th century monks' toilet (reredorter)

Below: the 12th century monks' toilet (reredorter).

Later reredorter 10 (Later toilet block)

The new toilet block was an impressive building measuring 51m (167 feet) by 10m (33 feet) and stood 7m (23 feet) high. It provided at least 59 cubicles, all at first floor level giving quick and easy access from the dormitory. A new sewer, with wooden sluice gates at the east end, ran along inside the building. The sewer was at the end of a system which ultimately flowed out to the east into the river estuary. Ingeniously the construction and route of this sewer meant that it could be flushed by the tidal flows of the river Ouse. In many reredorters wooden shutters were placed across the windows, but here at Lewes fragments of glass found in excavations suggest that the windows may have been glazed. The later construction of six huge buttresses against the southern wall of this building, and two more at the north-west corner, reveals that flooding and waterlogged ground were causing the walls to subside. When the Priory was demolished in 1538 this substantial building was saved and later used as a malthouse.

Frater 11 (Refectory)

Not much survives today of the frater building except for part of its basement. The monks ate their meals in silence in the dining room upstairs. They listened to a fellow monk give readings from the Bible or pious works from a raised pulpit. Their diet appears to have been healthy but frugal. Cluniac monks were allowed more food than the Rule of St Benedict prescribed because they spent more time in church. The Priory gardens and orchards 36 provided beans, peas, onions and fruit and herb gardens 25 supplied culinary and medicinal herbs. Grain was obtained from crops produced in the Priory's numerous granges and estates, and its mills turned the grain into flour to provide sufficient bread for all the monks, guests and servants. There would have been enough left over for charitable donations to the poor and needy who queued up at the gatehouse 18. A brewhouse 33 brewed beer, the normal everyday beverage along with wine.

Monks were allowed to eat meat on certain days of the year, but in periods of fasting and abstinence fish and dairy produce were the staple diet. When rules were later relaxed meat was more commonly eaten. Cheese, butter and eggs were regularly consumed. The Priory used fish from its well-stocked ponds 27, supplemented with locally caught fish, ducks and geese from the river Ouse and the sea. The Priory accounts also refer to swans. These would have been a luxury item and could have graced the prior's table on special occasions. Archaeological records show porpoise bones were found at the Priory which suggests they were eaten on occasion. The Priory's estates furnished quail and pheasants and other birds for the table. Rabbits were also bred for consumption. During one year in the 1530s the monks ate 171 oxen, 706 sheep and 83 pigs produced on the Priory's estates.

The Cloister 2

North of the present railway line lay the cloister, the chapter house 5 and the Great Church 1. In the cloister monks could enjoy peace and tranquillity for contemplation, prayer and study. The grassed central area (garth) was surrounded by a colonnade with elaborately carved capitals. The monks washed their hands in a large, ornate, circular, raised lavatorium (washing basin) 3 before entering the refectory. The lavatorium was probably fed from an underground bee-hive shaped chamber which still survives below ground on land just north of the present railway. A doorway gave access from the cloister directly into the Great Church.

Seal of the Priory of St Pancras, from the late 14th century. It shows, at the base, the martyrdom of St Pancras and the arms of de Warenne
© Trustees of the British Museum

The Chapter House 5

The chapter house lay on the east side of the cloister. This was the most important building in the Priory apart from the church. All the monks assembled here every day. A chapter from the Rule of St Benedict was read out and the day-to-day running of the community was discussed and agreed. With so much land and so many churches and with its obligations to Cluny there was much work to do. Letters had to be written, charters and leases drawn up, donations acknowledged, payments authorised, contracts signed and witnessed. All had to be sealed with the official seal. It was in the chapter house that monks confessed their faults and received punishment, including flogging and even imprisonment at Lewes or another Cluniac priory.

The chapter house with the dormitory above

19

ANDY GAMMON 2010

The chapter house was also a place for the burial of important people, and it was here that the remains of William de Warenne and his wife Gundrada were reburied. Other members of his family were also buried here up to the beginning of the 13th century. Many tombs were destroyed at the dissolution when just a few were rescued, among them the elaborate tomb of Richard, earl of Arundel. He was buried in the chapter house, in 1376 and his tomb was later placed in Chichester cathedral where it inspired the Philip Larkin poem, *An Arundel Tomb* (written in 1956). The exceptional monumental brass which covered the tomb of Prior Nelond, who died in 1432, was also saved from destruction and can now be found in St Peter's Church, Cowfold in West Sussex. The vast stone slab on which this brass is mounted was probably transported by boat down the river Ouse, along the coast to Shoreham and up the river Adur to complete the final stage of the journey by wagon.

The Prior's lodgings and kitchen c1520

Detail from the exquisite brass of Thomas Nelond, the 25th Prior, now in St Peter's Church Cowfold
Lewes Priory Trust

Tomb of Richard, Earl of Arundel and his wife Eleanor, originally placed in the Priory's chapter house, now in Chichester Cathedral
Image reproduced with the kind permission of Chichester Cathedral

The Prior's Lodgings 13, 14,15 19

On the western side of the cloister 2 (near modern housing) stood the prior's lodgings and his guest house. The prior's lodgings were both extensive and impressive as he needed to entertain important visitors and dignitaries, including representatives from the pope and from Cluny, as well as royal officials and members of the nobility. When Henry VIII's chief minister Thomas Cromwell acquired the monastery in 1538 he found this whole range of buildings sufficiently comfortable to be retained as a home for his son and family and to accommodate the king on a planned visit to Lewes, though this was cancelled on account of the plague.

The Hospitium 16 (Guest House)

The hospitium was a guest house for the less important visitors and was in existence by 1202. It was converted into a chapel when a new hospitium 17 was built (by 1260) and later became part of the parish church of St John the Baptist, in Southover. Some 12th century pillars and arcading to the nave still remain from the original hospitium.

The extensive prior's lodgings at Wenlock, a Cluniac Priory in Shropshire   muba

Gundrada's tomb

Southover church is well worth a visit. It is now the resting place of the founders of the Priory. In 1845 workmen building the Brighton to Lewes railway (which cuts right across the Priory site) discovered two small lead boxes (cists) inside which were the bones of William de Warenne and Gundrada. This discovery captured the imagination of the Victorians and prompted reports in local and national newspapers including the Illustrated London News for 1845. The interest aroused locally was instrumental in the founding of the Sussex Archaeological Society, in whose journals articles and excavation reports associated with the history of Lewes and its Priory can be found. The two lead boxes, which have the names of the founders engraved on them, now lie in the small chapel built onto the south side of Southover church to house them. The founders' remains themselves are buried under the grave slab on the floor of the chapel. This slab once adorned Gundrada's tomb in the Priory. It is one of the finest pieces of Romanesque carving to survive in England or even in Europe, exquisitely carved from Tournai marble blackened with wax or resin. In 1775 the slab was brought back to Southover from Isfield church, six miles north of Lewes, where Edward Shurley, who died in 1558, had used it for his own tomb.

The Remains of Gundrada and William.
R H Nibbs Oct 29th 1845
Sussex Archaeological Society Barbican House

The Tournai marble tomb slab of Gundrada, now in St John the Baptist Church, Southover. Horsfield after Lambert
Sussex Archaeological Society Barbican House

Herb Garden 25

Almost certainly adjacent to the infirmary there was a garden which grew the herbs needed for medicines. These were grown in raised beds made of planking, stone or wattle, which were easier to maintain and provided good drainage. A reconstruction of a herb garden can be seen adjacent the infirmary and is based on an idealised but detailed and scaled plan of such a herb garden taken from a 9th century manuscript depicting the monastery of St Gallen, in Switzerland. It records the dimensions of such a garden and names the herbs and plants to be grown. Medieval manuscripts and herbals, as well as more recent archaeological discoveries, provide other information to support this reconstruction.

Left: **Comfrey**
Used as a treatment for burns, abscesses and bruises. The root was crushed and used for dressing broken bones. An alternative name for the herb was knitbone.

Right: **Soapwort**
The roots of this plant made a kind of soap, used by the monks to wash themselves.

The present herb garden was constructed in the 1980s with the help of pupils from the nearby and appropriately named Priory School. Since that time many other individuals, societies and organisations, including Southover School, have helped to maintain and develop it.

Left: **Good King Henry**
A culinary herb. It was often mixed with nettles, sorrel and other greens and stewed to make a filling for a pie.

Right: **Lavender**
The flowers made an infusion to treat insect bite and sunburn, and to repel head-lice. Lavender flowers were also used in cooking.

Andy Gammon

The Infirmary 22

Elderly and sick monks were cared for in an enormous building, the infirmary. Nothing now remains above ground of its aisled hall 44.2m (145 feet) x 19.2m (63 feet). This was partially excavated at the beginning of the 20th century and further archaeological work in 2010 has confirmed the size of the building. The outline, laid out between the modern herb garden and the original toilet block, shows how large it was. The infirmary had beds in bays, perhaps later in cubicles, along its side aisles. The building was heated to provide some warmth in winter and had its own kitchens and toilets. The Rule of St Benedict, which formed the regulations for the Priory, allowed for sick monks in the infirmary to be given a different, more nourishing diet. Medicines would have been prepared following recipes preserved since antiquity in herbals (books containing descriptions and illustrations of plants to assist the keeper of the infirmary) and using herbs from the herb garden 25. Blood-letting, it was believed, improved your health. If a monk felt he would benefit from a session of blood-letting he would ask permission at the daily chapter house meeting and if it was granted the procedure would be carried out. The treatment involved the application of leeches to the body, or incisions made into the veins to release a flow of blood into a basin. Afterwards a short period of convalescence in the infirmary was allowed. Blood-letting seems to have become a social as well as a medical occasion as monks in the infirmary were not only allowed to eat meat but also to converse. The infirmary was only used for the treatment of monks at the Priory, not for the people of Lewes.

Archaeologist unearths a grave on the infirmary site. Sussex Express

Priory hospitals

The Priory maintained two hospitals outside the precinct walls. St James 43 was located just beyond the Priory walls in Southover opposite what is now Grange Gardens. Only the chapel of this hospital now survives, converted into a small cottage which is now in private hands. This chapel measured a mere 10.3m (34 feet) x 4.6m (15 feet). The infirmary which it served has gone but originally extended from the site of this chapel to the far end of St James Street. The second hospital, dedicated to St Nicholas, originally housed lepers and was situated at the western end of the town. Its location is preserved in the name Spital Road.

The hospital of St James, 1785. S. Hooper
Sussex Archaeological Society Barbican House

The chapel of St James' Hospital with detail of window

Priory Precinct

The Priory's walled precinct of about 15.7 hectares (39 acres) contained a number of ancillary buildings, including a brewhouse 33, a fish house 26 (by the fishponds 27), stables 38,40, a water mill 31, workshops, a forge 32 and a barn 39. A large pigeon house 30 (in the area that is now the grounds of the sports club) provided additional food. It survived until 1804 and reportedly had recesses for 3228 birds.

The whole precinct would have bustled with activity. Masons, builders and craftsmen were engaged at various times in construction and repairs to the Priory. Local people worked in the gardens and orchards 36 and transported goods in and out through the gatehouse 18 along the streets of Southover. They were also employed as servants in the prior's lodgings 13 and kitchens 12,14 and to unload boats at the riverside wharf 28 south of the reredorter 10. At the time of the dissolution 80 servants were employed by the Priory. It is difficult today to imagine the activities, the noise, the colour and the smells that would have originated from this extensive site and its numerous buildings.

Water Mill

Forge

Some of the precinct buildings as they may have looked c1520

Great barn

Pigeon House

Brewery

The Mound

To the east of the site near to the Dripping Pan entrance there is a large mound, the purpose and date of which has been the subject of much debate and speculation. Whatever its original purpose, the visitor to Priory Park today can obtain an excellent view of the whole area from its summit, including the land to the north of the railway and a view of Lewes Castle and the town.

The Great Gate 18

The whole of this monastic site was surrounded by a wall with entry at the north of the site through an impressive gatehouse, complete with battlements and rooms on the upper floor. Its main entrance was wide enough for horses and carts and was flanked by a side gate for pedestrians. Part of the gatehouse still survives, re-positioned in the 1830s at the west end of Priory Crescent in Southover. At the same time remains of the monks' cemetery were uncovered nearby. Contemporary accounts tell the gruesome story of how workmen sold parts of the skeletons they had uncovered. For sixpence you could purchase a 'jaw bone with a good set of teeth'. Dentures were often made of human teeth.

A surviving part of the Great Gate

The Great Gate, West view of the Priory Gateway, 1785. James Lambert
Sussex Archaeological Society Barbican House

Dissolution and destruction

'Lanzo's Cross' A cross made of walrus ivory from the 11th century found near the Priory in 1851. It was probably attached to a book and has a cavity at the back to hold a relic such as a piece of the True Cross. The hand of God descends to touch Christ's halo.
© The Trustees of the British Museum

Various building works were still in progress when the religious and political upheaval of the 1530s brought the life of the Priory to an abrupt end. In 1535 Richard Layton, one of Thomas Cromwell's royal commissioners, visited the Priory. He reported 'serious failings' including corruption and 'treasonable offences'. Whether these allegations were true or not it is impossible to say. In 1536 Parliament passed a law dissolving the smaller monasteries in England and Wales. Fearing the worst, in November 1537 Lewes's prior, Robert Crowham and the monks "voluntarily" signed the surrender of the Priory to the government. While elsewhere in the country abbots were executed for opposing the dissolution, Robert Crowham was able to secure valuable offices including appointment as treasurer of Chichester cathedral. The fate of most of the 24 monks is known. They were granted pensions or accepted appointments as priests in Sussex. The dissolution of the major monasteries was confirmed by the act of 1539.

Photograph showing a surviving leaning wall of the Great Church: evidence of Portinari's demolition technique.

Right: view looking north. W. Scott, c1770
Sussex Archaeological Society Barbican House

View looking east. James Lambert Snr., 1776
Sussex Archaeological Society Barbican House

Early in 1538 the Priory passed into the hands of Thomas Cromwell and the destruction of the religious buildings began. The Italian engineer Giovanni Portinari arrived from London with a gang of seventeen men to carry out this work. They did this by undermining the walls and setting fires. The physical evidence to support Portinari's description of exactly how this massive feat was achieved so quickly can best be seen in the remains of the first church. Here the angle of the surviving walls shows how they were brought down. Lead from the roof was melted down on site in purpose-built portable furnaces, while the Caen and Quarr stone and flints were loaded onto carts, or barges at the quayside, and removed for re-use elsewhere in Lewes and its vicinity. Many of the stones were re-used in houses in Lewes and can still be seen, most notably at Southover Grange. The site reverberated as the huge towers and walls crashed to the ground. The precinct must have resembled a vast reclamation yard, as the contractors sorted through the material and set about its disposal. Surprisingly there is no record of any disturbances or protests by the local population against the destruction of the Priory.

The Priory was looted and graves were smashed and robbed. Relics or shrines that had not already been destroyed, or secretly stashed away were now considered valuable pickings for the demolition squad. One such item that they appeared to have missed (or perhaps dropped in their haste to complete their work), is 'Lanzo's cross', which may have come from the cover of a book or have formed part of a reliquary. It is now in the British Museum. At the dissolution the Priory's collection of books would have been dispersed. A few might have been taken by the monks as they left the relative security of their monastery but sadly most would have been destroyed, their precious stones and jewels prised from their covers with little or no regard for the real literary treasures contained inside.

View of Lewes Priory and Castle, 1757. Samuel and Nathaniel Buck.
With three labeled details   Sussex Archaeological Society Barbican House

The Great Oven   The Frater

The 12th Century Reredorter

After the Dissolution

Portinari had systematically demolished the religious buildings but those structures that could be sold were saved from demolition and put to new uses, as we have seen with the prior's lodging and the later toilet block. In 1540, following the execution of Thomas Cromwell, the lease of the Priory passed to Nicholas Jenney. In the later sixteenth century the site was owned by Thomas Sackville, Earl of Dorset. The prior's lodgings, re-modelled as Lord's Place, later passed through marriage to John Tufton, the Earl of Thanet, whose son sold the house in 1688. By then its condition was described as 'ruinous .. and for the most part fallen downe and lying waste'. There is evidence that what remained was pulled down after 1688. An early 17th century lease refers to a 'saffron garden' at the site. The production of English saffron is well documented and it was sometimes cultivated for its medicinal uses (particularly for stomach ailments) and as a valuable dye.

A succession of owners of the Priory and its surviving remains did nothing to preserve this important site and by the early 19th century all above-ground traces of the church and chapter house had disappeared. Much of the south wall of the infirmary still existed in the mid 18th century but it too had gone by 1800, with the stone carted away. Later engravings show the ruins in various stages of decay and the land used for grazing, but the site still attracted visitors. A small Victorian folly in the form of a tower was constructed of Priory stone close to the entrance to a tunnel which allowed access from the southern to the northern part of the site now bisected by the railway line.

The preservation of what remains of the Priory is due to the hard work and dedication of many individuals including the architect Walter Godfrey and his son Emil who was instrumental in founding the Lewes Priory Trust. Various organisations have worked closely with Lewes Priory Trust including Lewes Town and District Councils, East Sussex County Council, The Heritage Lottery Fund, English Heritage and the Federation

Stones from the Priory reused at Southover Grange

of Cluniac Sites. It is hoped the renewed public interest and involvement in the site and the creation of Priory Park will lead to further excavation work and research, and thus an increase in our knowledge and understanding of the Priory of St Pancras and its local, national and international importance to ensure that this unique and precious site is preserved for future generations.

Visitors examine the remains of Gundrada and William de Warenne as navvies dig out the railway cutting in 1845. D Mossman and W.E. Baxter
Sussex Archaeological Society Barbican House

Underlay: a plan showing the path of the railway cutting through the foundations of the east end of the church, the chapter house, the cloister and the refectory. John Parsons, 1847
Sussex Archaeological Society Barbican House

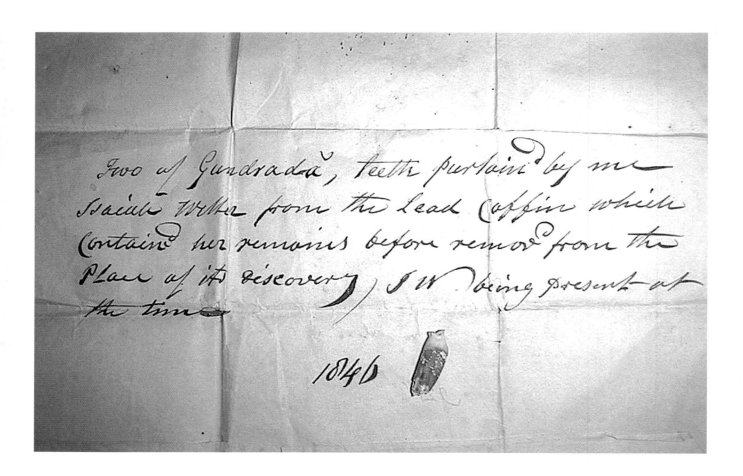

Two of Gundrada's, teeth pertain'd by me Isaiah Welke from the lead Coffin which Contain'd her remains before remov'd from the Place of its discovery) J W being present at the time

1846

East Sussex Record Office ACC 8648/37/12